Table of Contents

INTRODUCTION

The data in this book depends on the fruitful crate training strategy. Crate training isn't brutal. I rehash: Crate training isn't cruel. If utilized accurately, it uses the dog's natural lair intuition to your very own bit of leeway by urging the dog, not to pee or crap where it sleeps. Dogs usually are perfect creatures and will abstain from setting off to the bathroom where they sleep.

As I'm partial to stating, 'what goes in must turn out.' To enable you to figure out the best times to get your dog to go to the bathroom, it's essential to feed your dog at similar times each day. This is the perfect time to rehearse your house training lessons. For your dog's solace, it's additionally a smart thought to feed your dog in a similar place each day, a place that they will identify as their eating spot. With your puppy, there's a brief timeframe among eating and wiping out. Figure around 15 - 20 minutes. When feeding your dog, give her 15-20 minutes and after that, get the uneaten divide (if any). This will likewise instruct your dog to eat when encouraged. Once more, these principles can be loose once your dog is house trained yet, for the time being, it's critical to set up a daily schedule.

Until your dog is house trained, additionally keep away from treats and in the middle of supper snacks. The entire thought is to feed your dog, watch them always for the 15 - 20 minutes after they eat and afterward carry them to the place where you need them to do their business. Do it predictably, and you'll be setting your puppy in a position to succeed. This is tied in with setting desires and training your anxious student to do what you need. What's more, when they do, acclaim them fiercely. Make it appear that little pee or crap that they did is the best and most magnificent thing you've at any point found in all your years. Your companions and neighbors may believe you're insane. However, I can't pressure enough the intensity of recognition. It's what your puppy longs for. Give it to her in liberal sums.

How old should your puppy be before you start house training? Begin as ahead of schedule as you can, however, don't expect results until the puppy is around 14 weeks old. Before 14 weeks your little guy can't physically hold it in. At that point, why begin early you may inquire? Indeed, even though your little guy may not be physically ready to hold it in, she'll, at any rate, start realizing what's anticipated from her. Believe any training before 14 weeks to be 'pre-school.' When her physical capacities get up to speed with what you showed her, it will make it that a lot simpler to incorporate the lessons.

If you're thinking about crate training your dog as a method for house training, remember that the size of the container you pick is essential. A decent standard guideline about size is: the crate should be enormous enough for the dog to stand up and pivot in comfortably. You don't need the container so vast that the dog will mess toward one side and sleep at the other. For large-sized breeds that will keep on developing generously, you may need to purchase a more significant size later on if you plan for your dog to keep utilizing the crate after it is house trained. Also, the most basic standard of all: NEVER, under any conditions, use the container as a type of discipline. The crate ought to be where your dog needs to go, to sleep, and make tracks in the opposite direction from the clamor and action in your home. You never need them to connect it with being rebuffed.

CHAPTER ONE

Puppy Potty Training At Glance

Numerous people are hesitant to start training their dog at a young age. Frequently people believe that it's smarter to hold up until their puppy is more seasoned and mature before beginning training. Sooner you can start training your puppy the better. A puppy can respond to training from as young as around seven weeks old. This chapter outlines a portion of the issues engaged with training a puppy.

The primary thing to remember is that dogs are pack animals. In this way, your little puppy will quickly start attempting to work out his or her situation in their pack; i.e., your family unit. If you enable your puppy to manage the perch, you're giving out the message that the person is the pack leader. The more you allow your dog to remain in this fantastic position, it will be hard for you to declare your power once you choose to start attempting to train the person in question.

A few people feel that starting to train a puppy at a young age will remove the enjoyment of having a puppy. This isn't accurate because a significant part of the training techniques utilized for training puppies can be conveyed with regards to play. While playing, you have to hold up until your puppy displays a good bit of behavior. For instance, you might toss a toy for that person to pursue. If the person in question gathers this and offers it to you, this ought to be rewarded by a treat or heaps of praise. In the long run, you could present the direction 'get' to this game.

Remember that puppies have short focus ranges, much the same as youngsters. It's significant, consequently, to take training at your puppy's pace. If you start putting an excess of weight on your puppy to respond to directions, you may meet an obstruction.

It is additionally imperative to be true tolerance with your puppy. If you start getting crabby or forceful while training your puppy, you could wind up with an exceptionally anxious and eccentric dog. Attempt to disregard awful behavior (except if your puppy will accomplish something perilous) and center in around good practice. At first, all displays of good behavior ought to be rewarded.

A further critical component in training a young puppy is defining limits. You have to tell your puppy from beginning what behavior is satisfactory and what isn't. It's no utilization giving your puppy a chance to run frantic all around your home, jumping on everything in sight for a while, if this isn't how you need your dog to act in the long haul. If there is anything you don't need your dog to do, discourage this behavior from the start. Along these lines, for instance, if you don't need your puppy to get on specific household items, continue lifting that person down. If your puppy at that point approaches the furniture without jumping up on it - praise this behavior.

Puppy Training and Puppy Play - the Importance of Socialization

Puppy training is frequently extensively simpler than training a grown-up or pre-adult dog. One reason is that the puppy is a "clear record," untroubled by past training procedures and different issues. Another increasingly circuitous reason is that you are most likely bound to invest more energy and have more noteworthy persistence with your new puppy than you would after the "curiosity" has worn off somewhat. What's more, it will, in general, be human instinct to have more prominent tolerance with youthful (dogs and people), since we realize that they're unpracticed in life and they're typically anxious to learn.

In different ways, in any case, the puppy can be somewhat more challenging to prepare than a more established dog. One test to training another puppy is that little dogs are more effectively distractible than more established dogs. Everything is new to a puppy, and each unique experience gives another opportunity to diversion. Consequently, it is ideal to continue training sessions short when working with a puppy and to finish strong.

It is likewise critical to permit the puppy a lot of time to play and to cooperate with different pups and dogs. Socialization training is fundamental to making your new puppy a decent canine native, as dog hostility is a developing issue in numerous regions. Different dogs in the play gathering rebuff an appropriately mingled dog figures out how to play appropriately with different dogs and excessively forceful play.

This kind of play learning is something that occurs among kin in litters of doggies. As the dogs play with one another, they realize what is suitable and what isn't. Unseemly behavior, for example, hard gnawing or scratching, is rebuffed by different doggies, by the mother dog, or both.

Inability to appropriately mingle can be a noteworthy issue with your dog, and it is a significant reason for continually purchasing from a capable reproducer, and never taking your puppy home, he is eight weeks of age. An enormous extent of this considerable socialization experience happens in those last weeks with the puppy's mom and kin.

A capable and experienced raiser knows this, and will never permit forthcoming puppy owners to take doggies home until eight weeks of age, however it is by the by a significant and valuable actuality to know about yourself.

Tragically, numerous doggies are expelled from their moms and sold or received before this socialization has wholly happened. In these cases, much like never before, puppy play sessions started by you are a significant piece of any puppy training session. Most great puppy preschool training projects give time in every session to this sort of dog collaboration.

Acquainting your puppy with new encounters and new areas is likewise a significant piece of puppy training. Showing your dog to be dutiful and responsive, even despite numerous diversions, is substantial when training dogs and young doggies.

One incredible approach to mingle your puppy both to new people and new dogs is to take it on an outing to your nearby pet store. Many real pet store chains, and some free ones also, enable pet guardians to bring their fuzzy youngsters, and these stores can be extraordinary spots for little dogs to become acclimated to new sights, sounds, and scents. You will need to ensure the store permits pets before heading over, and you will likewise need to keep the visits genuinely short, both for the good of your puppy and in light of the pet store faculty.

It is significant for puppy owners to structure their pet's condition with the goal that the puppy is rewarded for good behaviors and not compensated for other people. One genuine case of this is hopping on people. Numerous people accidentally pay this behavior since it tends to be charming. While the facts confirm that hopping can be adorable for a 10-pound puppy, it won't be so lovely when that puppy has developed into a 100-pound dog.

Snickering at your puppy, or giving any consideration to him whatsoever when he bounces up, will be deciphered as a reward by your puppy - he will discover that he will get attention from you when he does this. So be exceptionally mindful so as not to confound your puppy. There are two procedures for undesired behaviors - immovably saying "No" to your puppy, as well as overlooking the action. For "recurrent guilty parties," the overlooking technique works best, as it is conceivable that your puppy will be deciphering ANY attention (even you saying "No" to him) as a reward for the behavior.

On the other hand, high behaviors ought to be rewarded quickly (either with treats or basically with bunches of attention and complain - saying "Great kid" in an extremely positive manner of speaking, and stroking your dog simultaneously is frequently similarly also gotten as treats seem to be). This kind of uplifting feedback will bring about a respectful grown-up dog that is an esteemed individual from both the family and the network on the loose.

The encouraging feedback technique can likewise be utilized in potty training the new puppy. Showing a puppy to use a remarkable surface, for example, rock or black-top is a decent procedure. The hypothesis is that the puppy will connect this surface with going potty, and in this manner be hesitant to utilize different surfaces (like your kitchen carpet, for instance) as a potty. Numerous young doggies can, with a little persistence, be promptly prepared to utilize a similar spot for toileting. This is an extraordinary strategy, as it will make your puppy to go "on order," and will spare you scouring the back yard when tidying up after your puppy.

An Effective Puppy Training

There are not many things in life as magnificent as a puppy. These little packages of vitality are as adorable as can be, and they draw out the best in us. They can give a lifetime of companionship and even show our youngsters obligation as they figure out how to think about another animal. It very well may fulfill transform that over the top wad of vitality into a respectful and faithful companion. To do this, all dog owners need to invest a specific measure of energy in puppy training.

It is critical to perceive that occasionally, doggies require expert guidance from an accomplished acquiescence coach. They are valuable in circumstances where a proprietor can't put much time in training, or when there is a specific issue that home training hasn't made a difference. It's likewise significant for your pet to get legitimate veterinary consideration with the goal that they are as sound as can be and are best arranged to learn.

For your pet's wellbeing, just as your family's security, there are a few commands that must be adopted immediately. For example, doggies usually bite and chew on things as they play. Directly from the begin, they should be prepared to not nip at family individuals. While it might be adorable and smooth now, as the dog develops, it might wind up perilous for this sort of play to proceed. It's ideal to start to get out from under the gnawing propensity the day they get back home.

Another area of training that is significant is showing the puppy that the general population in the home are the ones who are in command of them. Tell it there are areas where it is permitted, and different spots it isn't. Having a crate accessible is an incredible method to accentuate this. Your pet will discover that it is alright for it to be in its container, yet not on the sofa, for example.

An essential snippet of data for a puppy to learn is the "come" command. It is risky for pets to run free. Even under the least favorable conditions it could be lost or harmed, or, best-case scenario, it could trouble other individuals by meandering somewhere it isn't greeted. Neither one of the options is adequate, so this is a hugely significant thing for your pet to learn.

A part of the training that additionally needs to be tended to quickly is housebreaking. It is significant for the soundness of your pet and for everybody in the family that the puppy has a spot to take out its losses in the best possible area. This is a challenging and lengthy procedure some of the time. Here is another area where the crate will be massively useful, as creatures will as a rule not kill where they rest.

There are numerous sources to use to become familiar with the ideal approaches to prepare a puppy. Also, different techniques may work superior to others for a specific pet. There are numerous books on dog training accessible, and websites offer advice. You might almost certainly discover free or minimal effort training courses at pet food stores or accommodating social orders. Additionally, proficient mentors are always accessible for those occasions you need them.

Creatures advance our lives as they become adored increments to our families. Significantly, our pets are prepared and prepared appropriately with the goal that they remain sheltered and glad. With a little direction, your dog can be ready to be as well as can be expected to be as they amuse us with their friendship and energetic nature.

Sheltered and reliable dog training is something that is paid attention to very. Permit these amicable dog training Calgary masters to prepare your dog or puppy. The educated staff will help shield your little kids and furniture by instructing compliance to your pet.

Puppy potty training isn't advanced science, yet it requires learning, commitment, and a great deal of persistence. It's likewise significant that you don't commit some common and effectively avoidable errors. The accompanying rundown of potty-training tips was incorporated to give you a review of potty training as a rule and to fill in as a snappy reference when you have some specific inquiry.

Without squandering any additional time, we should go directly to...

Puppy Potty Training

Puppies more youthful than eight weeks of age are too young to be in any way potty prepared. Simultaneously, the more you hold up following eight weeks, the more drawn out and progressively difficult housebreaking will be.

A customary sustaining and strolling timetable will make potty training puppies much less stressful.

When your puppy chaotic heaps up, and it will occur on numerous events, except if you got him in the demonstration, tidy up and be increasingly careful whenever. Upbraiding is fine, however just if you got him in the exhibit. Regardless, never hit or shout at your puppy. He won't comprehend why you are doing that, and the main thing he will learn is to fear you.

The exact inverse of the past puppy potty training tip, each time your puppy wipes out where he should acclaim him. By and large, puppies are anxious to satisfy us. If they see that something, they did meets us, they will attempt to rehash similar conduct later on.

Need to housebreak your puppy in the briefest time conceivable? Consider case training. No other sort of puppy training offers the same number of advantages.

This is most likely the least demanding puppy potty training tip to pursue - never overload or "overdrink" (sorry, couldn't locate a superior term!) your puppy, particularly before his bedtime. You'll be stunned what number of individuals commit this error!

Try not to squander your time paper training your puppy. All it will achieve is to show your puppy that it's OK to wipe out inside. You will likewise have a lot harder time "unteaching" this conduct later on.

If your puppy will stay home for expanded timeframes, think about instructing him to utilize a litter box. It offers a much cleaner choice to paper training.

Puppy Training Tips & Information

Puppy training is one of the fun parts of having a puppy. You make a bond among you that will keep going for whatever length of time that you are as one and give the person in question the abilities essential to remain safe. Much the same as youngsters, we train hounds not to control them but rather to shield them from doing things that will hurt themselves, such as running into the road or eating something that will destroy them.

In addition, like youngsters, training a puppy is neither necessary nor straightforward and frequently baffling. Notwithstanding, with consistency and constancy, center and the correct techniques, it tends to be finished!

Here is the excellent puppy training education ought to include:

- Heel and sit
- Come and sit
- Down
- Remain

These fundamental commands will give your puppy the establishment for increasingly broad training later. However, how would you show a little, wiggly body how to be still for anything considerably fewer specific commands? You can discover a considerable number of different books and techniques, nearly as shifted as the breeds that will direct you on the tone your training should take. In any case, regardless of which one you pick, there are a couple of fundamental standards to puppy training that are basic to your prosperity.

Energy

Training includes control and order has negative implications in our general public, yet your puppy training need not be harmful to be compelling.

Keeping up a positive concentration and offering treats for proper execution and overplaying triumphs as opposed to investing a lot of energy when your puppy doesn't react accurately to the command is vital. This continues training time as a fun time for both of you and won't become a feared errand. Instead, your puppy will anticipate training time and will be excited for reacting to your commands such that fulfills you.

Keep It Short

Indeed, even the puppy with the longest attention span won't last longer than 10 minutes in a training session. Help both of you out and attempt to keep all your training sessions somewhere in the range of 5 and 10 minutes each. You may, in any case, complete a 30 minutes' worth of work ordinary, however, split it up. For instance, 5 minutes before you get down to business, 10 minutes when you return home, 5 minutes while dinner is preparing, and 10 minutes after dinner.

The redundancy in customary interims for short measures of time serve to imbue the new commands into your puppy's cognizance. He'll lift them a lot faster than if you attempted to go through 30 minutes training him once per day. Additionally, it's a lot simpler to get 5 minutes here, and 10 minutes there is a bustling timetable than to attempt to write in an entire 30-minute session every day.

Incorporate Others

Attempt to consolidate a portion of your puppy training sessions with occasions and individuals that will help mark the commands on the puppy's psyche. He ought to react to controls when they are spoken by others just as you. He ought to likewise respond to authorities when he truly needs to accomplish something different - like have dinner or pursued a ball.

Ensure that everybody who contributes to your puppy's training says the commands similarly and catches up with a similar reward framework and techniques. It will just confound your puppy to get different data from different relatives or to get one treat from one relative and three treats from another.

The most significant part of fruitful puppy training is fun! Have a good time and your puppy will make the most of his practice, getting energized when it's time to 'perform.'

Keys to Puppy Training

A significant component in puppy training is socialization. If your dog is expertly mingled, they will almost certainly interact with different people and creatures without being alarmed or feel they have to utilize dynamic behavior. Else, it may be essential to restrict your dog to the house all the ideal opportunity for his wellbeing and others. During the initial three months of young doggies, life is significant for teaching socialization skills a while later, and it is vital to strengthen and improve these skills.

Leash training and obedience training is vital in training your puppy to address the behavior. Make sure that your puppy is fitted appropriately with a neckline and after that get him acquainted with a leash. The neckline should fit cozy yet not firmly. Training your puppy to a leash will allow the puppy to stroll in outside settings. Obedience training will show your puppy to react to directions and keep the puppy from utilizing negative behavior.

Some fundamental tips can help the achievement of most puppy training methods. You should utilize positive reinforcement when training your puppy. When your puppy pursues directions remunerate him with recognition or treats. Positive reinforcement can assist the puppy with bettering to comprehend the training. Beginning your practice in a tranquil situation free from distractions can make the preparation simpler on you just as your puppy. Housebreaking, your puppy will require persistence and comprehension to wind up productive.

A typical error made by pet proprietors is chiding their doggies when it is past the point of no return. Past the point of no return implies when you didn't get him in the act. If you shout or reprove your puppy sometime later will befuddle him. If your puppy makes a mess and you didn't get him in the law tidy up the mess without creating an object. If you do get him in action distract him with a noisy "NO" and rapidly take him outside while he is sincerely busy eliminating. At that point, after he has done his business in the right region acclaim him. Try not to shame puppy with nose in his mess. In addition to the fact that this is pitiless, it might make him scared of eliminating before you.

This will cause issues he will, at present, take out in the house at the same time, will attempt to cover up to do it. This could likewise make him eat his mess in dread of how you will react. Housebreaking your puppy must not have migraines if you go about it entirely. Persistence, timing, and consistency are the keys to adequately housebreaking your puppy. Loads of gestures of recognition and prizes and great demeanor will come ways.

CHAPTER TWO

Dog Training: Should You Start Puppy Training Early?

Numerous people need to begin dog training right away because the puppy may do things that are not exactly attractive, or they think it is an extraordinary way to bond with their new puppy. In any case, your young dog ought to have some opportunity until it's around 4 to a half year old before getting into formal dog training. In any case, that doesn't mean you are not beginning some training.

Presently, because you're not officially training your dog does not mean you shouldn't try to begin early puppy training with just lessons like how to act around other people. It's essential to purchase a well-fitting neckline and leash, at that point use them when you're out in open spots. This is for both different people's advantage just as your own. You wouldn't need your puppy to all of a sudden run out into the center of a bustling road. let's say the Truth, you may find that there is a leash law in your city that restricts letting any dog run free including young doggies and when you go to a recreation center or other open spots you need to ensure your puppy is near you. Your puppy training now is increasingly casual as you are teaching your puppy to stroll on a leash.

You need to ensure that your puppy is getting sufficient opportunity to play outside and every day work out. Exercise is the ideal way to ensure that his bones and lungs are getting solid. You need to pursue at any rate 20 minutes per day of giving your puppy a chance to go around the yard. One fun way of joining both puppy training and practicing your puppy is to get him to pursue you around the yard. You are teaching him to pursue his pack head and concentrating on you at this young age. Doing this will make dog training simpler later on.

Formal Puppy Training:

When your puppy is more than four months old, you can start formal dog training. It is ideal to begin at this young age because more seasoned dogs stall out in their ways and are much harder to prepare. That doesn't mean you start with the hardest piece of training with these your ones, and you need to begin puppy training with only ten minutes per day.

Young doggies can get worn out rapidly and will lose center. Your puppy won't be any to deal with a great deal of puppy training from the start. Ensure these sessions are on an ordinary calendar of working a little with him consistently. This normal will demonstrate your puppy that you are not kidding about these puppy training lessons. An additional stunt you can attempt is to wear similar shoes or coat, so your puppy builds up a relationship with these things of apparel and his training sessions.

Training Your Puppy to Heel

1. One of the most significant aptitudes in puppy training is figuring out how to Heel. You will need to have your puppy prepared to wear a neckline and alright with a leash before beginning to make him Heel. The initial segment of training your puppy to Heel is to have your puppy stroll nearby you on the left-hand side.
2. Slap your thigh and state HEEL now and then to urge your young dog to tail you and keep beside you during the training session. Your puppy may get diverted or not pursue your lead from the start, however, continue strolling, and your little guy will begin to get it.
3. When your puppy begins to tail, you compensate the conduct by revealing to him a great dog. Work on heeling each day during your puppy training sessions; thus, your puppy will heel next to you.

Teaching Your Puppy to Sit

1. Teaching your puppy to sit is a fundamental ability for puppy training. To begin, have a little bit of treat in your hand.
2. Hold the treat close to your young doggies' nose and move it in

reverse over his head. Tenderly press down with your other hand on his back and manage him into a sitting position. As you press down during the puppy training session guide him to sit in a firm voice.

3. Rehash this procedure a few times during the puppy training sessions and make sure to laud your puppy each time he finishes the activity. Teaching a puppy to sit is perhaps the least demanding direction, however one of the more import directions that you'll use during the majority of your puppy training lessons.

Dog Training - Learn Something about Dog

Numerous individuals accept that dog training is hard. Numerous additionally allow that a few dogs are necessarily not trainable. Both of these perspectives aren't right. Without a doubt, training a dog can be enjoyable. Some dog breeds are more uncomplicated to prepare more than others. What we cannot help contradicting, nonetheless, is the declaration that there are dogs which can't be ready - because that is not true. What we are to investigate at the point, are a portion of the things you have to do, to get the training of your dog right.

Parameters for checking success

You'll be regarded to have gotten the training of your dog right if you figure out how to pass on the essential dog skills to your pooch inside a sensible measure of time.

You'll further be regarded to have gotten the training of your dog right if you figure out how to the essential dog skills in a suffering area. This is to say that you won't be viewed as having been successful in training your dog if the pooch overlooks the skills instructed inside multi-day.

In this way, more or less, the parameters through which success in dog training can be measured include:

- The length of time consumed in passing on the essential skills to the dog.
- The skills instilled in the dog.
- How long the dog holds the skills.

Iif you are taking too long to even think about passing on specific skills to the dog, if you think that its challenging to instill individual talents in the dog, or if the dog continues overlooking skills instructed to the person in question, it doesn't really imply that you aren't doing things well. You need to remember is that the two factors are affecting everything here. The first of those is your skill, bent, and commitment as a dog trainer. What's more, the second of those is your dog's average capacity - against a foundation where some puppy breeds appear to 'get' things quicker than others.

Early inception as the key to success in the training dogs

There is a little skill that you can instruct to a dog when someone in question is so youth. The accepted way of reasoning that little dogs underneath a half year of age shouldn't be prepared inside and out wrong. There are a few skills you'll discover hard to educate to a dog that is more seasoned than a half year. It is essential that not at all like us people, dogs are (here and there) profoundly advanced creatures - whose life skills learning procedure begins the minute they are conceived. That is why a little dog that loses his mom at a quarter of a year of age might most likely make due in the wild.

Presently the best time to begin training a dog would be when the individual in question is learning fundamental life skills, with the goal that the skills you need to pass on to the person in question are likewise received close by those essential canine life skills. That way, the required behaviors would be a piece of the dog's character.

The right utilization of rewards and revisions as the key to success in training dogs.

While we get to the quick and dirty of dog training, it develops that different skills and behaviors must be transmitted and imbued in dogs through the right utilization of rewards and remedy.

The highest reward you can provide for a dog is attention. What's more, on the other hand, the enormous remedy/discipline you can provide for a dog is the hardship of care.

In this manner, if you need to get your dog to pick a specific behavior, you have to recreate (or instead show) it to that person, and after that reward the person in question (with attention) when he acts in like manner, whist likewise rebuffing the person in question (with hardship of care) when or she neglects to act appropriately. Merely taking a gander at the dog affectionately is a way of 'rewarding' the person in question with attention. Petting the someone in question is another type of attention reward. Applauding the pooch verbally is one more way of rewarding that person with care. Genuine, the dog may not comprehend the words, yet the person can detect the feelings behind them. A dog appears to have that capacity.

In the meantime, if your dog was making the most of your attention while accomplishing something right and you deny the person in question of that attention the minute the individual begins performing something incorrectly, he in a split second detects the response and makes the association between his misbehavior and the hardship of care. He is slanted to address the behavior to recover your attention. These things work exceptionally well if the dog you are attempting to prepare is as yet youthful.

What you mustn't do, nonetheless, is to hit the dog as a type of discipline/amendment: the fundamental reason being that the dog won't comprehend that being hit is a type of 'discipline.' Instead, the hit pooch will accept that you are merely brutal to the person in question. If the dog continues doing things like racing to the street or destroying neighbors' stuff, you'd be better instructed to discover ways concerning restraining his developments, as opposed to hitting him.

Tolerance is the key to success in the training of dogs

You won't be successful in dog training except if you are tolerant. You need to remember is that it requires some investment to pick thoughts that appear to be excessively accessible to us as people. Some individuals have this confusion that you must be successful in dog training if you are 'intense.' unexpectedly, this is one of those undertakings where consideration and the 'delicate methodology' appear to work superior to the extreme Spartan way to deal with training.

Perseverance is the key to success in the training of dogs

Firmly identified with tolerance (as the key to success in dog training) is steadiness. You will not be successful as a dog trainer if you surrender too effectively - that is, similar to where you outline an ideal behavior to a dog, and after that surrender, if the dog neglects to lift it right away. The reality of the condition is that you need to represent a craving behavior to a dog a few times while utilizing the essential fortifications, till the dog, in the long run, comes to realize what is anticipated from the person in question.

Effective Communication in Dog Training

Dogs are stunning animals. They adjust to incalculable circumstances. They are sensational at affiliations: including learning the importance or ramifications of numerous sounds, for example, human language. A dog's "vocabulary" can arrive at upward of 150 particular words! But, paying little heed to how keen, how gifted, and how versatile they are, dogs will never be verbal animals. Their first language isn't words, yet body language. Along these lines, it's just regular that your dog will translate your words; however, a "channel" - facial expression, of body language, tone of voice, even your attention. Also, if at least one of these "deviant" with the words you are utilizing, most dogs will "comply" your body language!

As far as I can tell, most tangles in the dog training procedure result from miscommunication, not stubbornness, tenacity, or predominance. While this chapter is designed for training the family dog, the truth of the matter is that whether your dog is carefully a family pet, a rival in canine games or an all-day working dog, taking advantage of your training time means learning to discuss viably with your dog.

Communication Begins with Attention

Conceivably a principal type of communication is your attention. This is genuine whether you are teaching some new ability, rehearsing an old one, or refining a propelled behavior. When you pay seriousness to something your dog does - through touch, voice, eye contact, grinning, or giggling - you attract attention to the behavior. This tells your dog that you discover the action deserving of intrigue. Dogs, being friendly animals, find most communication and attention strengthening. They esteem it, and will work to get it - and this isn't notwithstanding thinking about whether the dog finds the behavior fortifying all by itself. So when training, remember that you don't need to reward practice for strengthening it adequately.

Bring yourself into a training session focused on focusing on your dog to a similar degree that you are requesting that he focus on you. Abstain from training when you are diverted or pre-involved. This is essential regard and thought, close to you would give any great companion! To be mindful to your dog, you don't need to gaze at him, yet you ought to know about him. A viable mentor knows, present, and "at the time" while training, prepared and ready to note and reward all significant reactions, as they occur.

What's more, if your dog gives a response, you weren't seeking after? Rather than drawing attention to it, verbally or something else, disregard it and proceed onward! Drawing attention to poor reactions frequently permanently concretes them in the dog's cerebrum and makes it almost sure that he will offer it once more. Focus your vitality and attention on behaviors you need to see once more.

As you practice this way to deal with working with your dog, you will before long find that your dog will work gain your attention by doing those things you like. As your dog's behavior consistently improves, voluntary cooperation builds, your association with your dog gets more grounded, and you both have a ton of fun training. Sort of elusive a drawback to that, wouldn't you say?

The Body Language of Effective Dog Training

Training your dog is a definitive expression of authority: you are stepping up to the plate and instruct, manage, and direct your dog. Your body language, in this way, ought to mirror your job as instructor and pioneer, conveying a quiet self-assurance and levelheadedness. How about we the goose at the parts of non-verbal communication as they influence your dog:

Let learning be invited with your facial expression and demeanor. Your body language starts at the top, with your face. Training should be a positive, charming knowledge for you and your dog. Before you start, and occasionally all through, intentionally loosen up your facial muscles. Smile tenderly. Mellow your eyes. Take a profound, loosening up breath, and continue relaxing! When you are loose and cheerful, you present a place of refuge for your dog's attention. (Furthermore, there is not something to be tense about, isn't that so? This is dog training, not world harmony!) A delicate eye will invite your dog to search out your face, though a hard gaze may threaten your dog into looking away, lessening your capacity to convey unmistakably.

If you wind up getting to be bothered, disappointed, tense, or on edge, you may find that your dog mirrors your feelings:

He may look for tranquility somewhere else, by abstaining from taking a gander at you, or notwithstanding attempting to move away from you. A few dogs become exaggeratedly moderate and quiet, or even show agreeable behaviors, as they try to quiet you.

He may "carry on" trying to occupy you or diffuse the circumstance. This kind of dog may turn out to be commonly disturbed, or even retreat to stupid jokes to hold you from yourself!

If you become anxious, numerous dogs will mirror that apprehension, either diverting themselves from an awkward circumstance or glancing around to discover the wellspring of your strain.

If any of these occur while training your dog, before you direct your dissatisfaction at him, look to yourself first. Take a deep, enduring breath, loosen up your face and your body, smile, and attempt once more!

Impart confidence. When training your dog, particularly a dog new to you or new to training, your developments and body language should radiate a demeanor of quiet, loosened up confidence. As much as is sensible, stay upstanding without being inflexible. (Keep in mind your facial expression? Your body language ought to likewise "invite learning.") When in doubt, an upright yet loosened up stance imparts confident expert - an excellent teaching stance. If your body needs to twist, keeping your shoulders generally back will help keep up a heading of confidence. While this is progressively significant with a dog starting its training, and with ordinarily unrestrained or self-assured characters, any dog can end up bewildered by a lot of bowing, bowing, dodging, and bouncing. He may generally expect that you are playing, acting accommodating, anything other than training! Any hand sign related with directions ought to be perfect, straightforward, and complete. They ought to be free from over the top, suitable for nothing movement, and ought to never be utilized to compromise or annoy the dog.

Convey self-restraint. Stay composed. No matter how whether you are working on a stationary exercise, (for example, a sit-remain), or a moving practice, (for example, behaving, or a review), focus on keeping your body language "calm." Try not to cover your cue in a spout of befuddling, negligible signals or movement. Enable your dog to focus on your words and any expected hand or body messages; don't set him in a place to need to sort the goods worth keeping from the refuse. When your dog is further developed in his training, you may wish to instruct him to react to verbal cues in spite of inconsequential body language. But, for the time being - first of all. Stroll before you run!

Something other than Words

Conveying unmistakably and viably to your dog incorporates getting to be mindful of how your tone of voice, and conveyance of cues, influence how your dog learns and reacts. When training your dog, remember that your voice passes on something other than the direction itself.

To start with, be reliable. Dog proprietors new to training frequently fluctuate their cue conveyance, exchanging forward and backward between, for instance, a decent, clear "sit," a loud and commanding "SIT!", and a sing-spongy, not especially confident-sounding "si-it?" To a dog, every one of these sounds is all together, dislike a similar cue by any means! Once more, dogs are not verbal animals. Conveying a direction that fluctuates in tone, pitch, and length can and will confound your training accomplice. Do yourself and your dog some help: keep the sound of your cues predictable. As such, pick a voice and be adapt to it.

Talk in a natural voice. As you give your cue, picture your dog playing out the exercise pleasantly - this confidence will come through in your voice. Maintain a strategic distance from whiny tones, addressing, or arguing. Attempting to prepare your dog in these "lost little dog" tones will be an exercise in dissatisfaction. They won't pick up your affirmation, substantially less regard! Keep in mind, and you are an educator, a mentor, a coach - not a worker. At the other outrageous, you don't need to accept a noisy, extreme sounding "order voice." This is for two reasons.

To begin with, forceful, threatening tones will in general present obstruction in progressively confident dogs, and unthinking subservience in less positive ones. Nor is helpful for learning, cooperation, or collaboration. Second, your dog is flawlessly fit for tuning in and reacting when you talk in a standard, beautiful, ordinary tone of voice. Expecting you intend to use what you've shown your dog in your regular day to day existence, you will train your dogs to a great extent throughout the day. Things being what they are, why on the planet show your dog that you need to play "military trainer" to have him do as you inquire? It brings extra worry into training, isn't exceptionally gainful, and positively doesn't mirror a relationship of willing organization. The truth of it is that your dog is considerably more liable to react serenely, eagerly, and insightfully if your voice and demeanor are loose and conversational. The main concern: to promote cooperation, show your dog his cues in a view that is sensible, agreeable, and normal for you.

Genuine thankfulness is critical. Very regularly, we get so made up for the lost time and focused on teaching our dogs that, exactly when we need to unwind and appreciate the snapshot of progress, we wind up giving empty praise, practiced, and in all honesty, not very praise-like by any stretch of the imagination. Remember that the words are not significant; it's your demeanor that matters. Praise doesn't need to have a specific tonal quality or pitch about as much as it needs to pass on that you are genuinely satisfied and glad right then and there. Your dog should feel genuinely refreshing for a vocation very much done - paying little heed to whether the achievement was a long looked for after quantum jump, or one of the many small steps to progress en route.

Don't hesitate to "trial" different cheerful sounds on your dog, to perceive what sort of response you get. In any case, once more, the most significant thing is that your dog knows, from your voice and your demeanor, that you are satisfied. Try not to figure you can trick your dog - he lives with you and is entirely mindful of how you sound and look when you are glad, pitiful, distracted, and indifferent. Rationally value your dog as you give your praise, and it will come through in your voice.

If you do need to utilize your voice to show that you don't need a specific behavior - regardless of whether you state no, or ah-ahh, wrong, and so forth - the sound ought to be pretentious, not angry or terrifying. The fact is to instruct, not threaten. Keep in mind, as you work with each other, both you and your dog will make mistakes. The effect of the matter isn't to make him feel gravely for his mix-up, yet to figure out how to best assist him to be correct. A dog prepared along these lines will comprehend your message while proceeding to need to work with you.

Assembling it All

Thus, when working with your dog, make up your brain to unwind, smile, be quiet, and have a great time. Would you be able to do it another way? Sure. Be that as it may, this chapter is tied in with helping you make the vast majority of your communication with your dog and expanding the adequacy - and satisfaction - of your training time. It's not just alright, and it's healthy and a not out of the ordinary piece of the learning procedure. Presently get out there and live it up!

Varieties of Effective Dog Training Methods

Individuals of different ages, youthful and old, will love having a dog or a little guy around. They even treat them as their closest companion. In any case, you should likewise think about the possible results that accompany owning one. Practical Dog Training is essential for your dog, and you ought to comprehend you need to try to mingle your dog. You need to open your dog to the outside world, with the goal that it won't scare other individuals.

There are dog-training techniques you can pursue with the goal that you can deal with it effectively, for example, dog murmuring, reward training, and clicker training. Knowing these techniques all will make Effective Dog Training simpler to oversee.

Regardless of many dog training methods to choose from, a few examples recorded here are sorted in the accompanying request:

1. ways depending on learning speculations as a representation of behavior control

2. methods depending on dog ethology, including typical or standard dog propensities or behavior.

Moreover, a few methods, as indicated by rehearsing speculations, which might be composed inside three particular subcategories:

one) Typical training of your dog (negative reinforcement)

two) Positive training

three) Mixed techniques.

Negative Dog training was initially first designed for war canines. This innovation was helpful in the occasions, paving the way to the first world war. This training method was used up via trainers who are regular citizens after the subsequent world war time frame, and rapidly had turned out to be set up as acknowledged ordinary practice.

Customary legitimate dog training or negative reinforcement

Punishment and negative reinforcement incorporate the fundamental instructing methodologies to conventional training.

Punishment, in any case, is an obnoxious reaction to a specific behavior. Although punishment could debilitate a practice, it surely isn't outright. Besides, such sentences routinely have undesired security impacts.

Positive articulation of reinforcement is a method that enables an outlook like a repulsive circumstance is maintained a strategic distance from as per the aftereffect of the one behavior.

By the method, for example, pushing on a canine's shoulders can create a repulsive encounter for your canine. If your weight behind him disappears whenever he is in a down position, your dog will effectively turn out to be all around prone to play out a similar activity inside the not so distant, to evade this sort of unpalatable sensation. This way, your fuzzy companion will connect the order of laying with the terrible affiliation or negative reinforcement.

Choke chains, prong collars and stun (electric) collars are ordinary devices in conventional training and its variations. Without a doubt, such practice is commonly equipped towards dog submission works out, ignoring behavioral issues.

One occasion of impugning could be in case of hitting your pet or yelling because your canine has climbed onto a rocker. Inevitably the final product is that you could likely influence your pet dog to jump from the comfortable chair; nonetheless, almost no real inevitability will guarantee that this climbing couldn't occur a subsequent time. Such unrequested results could work out with the goal that the canine may chomp you, become very scared upon your appearance or experience fears around comfortable chairs.

Promoters actualizing this method regularly feel that such thorough training offers reliable arrangements that can't be accomplished in different ways. What's more, they accept dog-training collars, for example, choke, stun and prong are not hurtful because canines have a genuinely great high resistance torment level.

Naysayers of such canine training accept that this method and dog-training gear included are pointlessly pitiless and uncouth and to be sure not extremely Effective Dog Training. Also, they receive such a procedure could conceivably cause hazardous security impacts, including apprehension gnawing and harm towards the trachea from the dog.

Positive canine-training

This canine-training framework has been fabricated gratitude to the standards of an operant molding framework created by Mr. Skinner. Although not a novel method, it just came into regular use during the nineteen nineties.

Positive dog-reinforcement is a very mainstream method. This sort of reinforcement occurs because of your canine's specific frame of mind. One example ought to be if one gives a sustenance reward to one's canine after they set down, they'll generally spread out regularly to get this sort of tasty treat. Subsequently, the dog will probably be seeing how to set somewhere around method for a positive dog-reinforcement approach.

On the other hand, if your canine should put itself down, and the next fifteen seconds is given a dog reward, your dog can disassociate the behavior of resting with the treat. Your doggie may trust you gave the award fundamentally because it was looking upwards, or there is a development from your dog's ears to signify intrigue. Along these lines, rewarding your canine companion was completed, yet by and by, the specific required behavior wasn't strengthened.

Clicker-training

Clicker-training typically is viewed similar to a mainstream dog-training method.

One difference that is undoubtedly prominent with clicker-training when contrasted and different methods are executing a clicker for that first example. The clicker is frequently a little device when a clicking sound hails from when it is pressed. This is done to take note of the total minute in the occasion the canine plays out a behavior.

Other such characteristics of these techniques are incredibly straightforward and pleasant to finish. Such methods aren't typically tons of compliance and famous for finding solutions for such behavioral issues.

The missing component of negative-based reinforcement, or punishment and collars for training, for example, choke, stun or prong can permit favorable canine training arrangements a route for the two canines and their proprietors. Such a component could well be the undeniable favorable position for such sorts of training.

Naysayers for these techniques select that canines prepared with positive methods won't wholly react if your dog can smell or sniff out a tasty treat.

Regardless of being so reasonable, such perceptions are false. Effectiveness of positive dog-training is then polished every day by many administration canines for disabled proprietors, or police canines, rivalry canines, and performing canines.

A blend of techniques actualizes both positive and negative reinforcement with the plan to accomplish a superior degree of Effective Dog Training.

While choke-collars appear to be all the more generally used, we can think about how the differed methods will, in general, be drawing in canines instead of conventional dog-training.

Blended training techniques

To be sure, the most pervasive response for the utilizing of the blending of relationship with such energetic behaviors, as an example, leaving the ambush sleeve, are difficult to grasp without the use of negative-based reinforcement.

Regardless of trainers who actualize an assortment of methodologies and furthermore use such positive kinds of reinforcement, regularly they typically avoid utilizing nourishment for reinforcement purposes. In the occasion the trainer needs to use a reinforcer of positive use, it tends on a tendency to choose games rather than sustenance as a reward.

A few methods to prepare are based upon dog ethology.

Ethology, a science usually viewed as based on concentrates from the behavior or species inside an individual circumstance. Typically, it could study intuitively or those that are not natural habitual behavior all things considered.

Methods that give dog ethology typically think about the canine's regular behavioral examples, however, usually disregard the nuts and bolts for the learnings of hypotheses.

Following the worldview or with pack leader, canines make prevailing progressive systems inside this pack. Hence, one must turn into the alpha or pack leader to keep up a warm relationship together with your canine.

The essential thought of methods based around technologies is consistent that the proprietor must wind up being the pack leader.

Although not quickly evident if the alpha concept started, we could believe that the eighties generally perceived the buzz on this concept. Cesar Millan and Jan Fennell would be the most renowned creators for these methods.

The following has turned into the unmistakable trainer, because of his "Dog Whisperer" show.

Different creators consider these techniques have establishments in scholastic examinations as indicated by studying the idea of packs of wolves. These techniques were additionally considered and executed after your various long periods of study from the behavior of canines.

Alone, they are ineffective to teach directions as indicated by dog submission. In this sense, a lot of trainers tend not to receive these genuine dog-methods.

For sure, it truly is a worry that those known for rehearsing these previously mentioned techniques don't consider themselves to be trainers. Truth be told their cases are of being people that can impart towards canines with a profound affirmation of a dog's non-verbal communication and behavior.

Lamentably, ethology-based methods differ from another, with there being no certain standard for their benefit. Without a doubt, a few ways appear comprising of just mainstream views and not on real examinations.

Insufficient enticing cases are made concerning such methods. Such methods can likewise be depending on the standard belief system, which might be the situation for various purposes for this kind.

Victors of such ethology-based methods believe these methods to be an ordinary procedure to ' talk' with canines. Such heroes likewise utilize increasingly obliging techniques. Such hostility levels in these methods are in all respects profoundly variable and depend upon the framework used by the dog-trainer.

Depreciators typically question the concept of an alpha dog leader and talk about as though there's little requirement for such hierarchical predominance.

Maybe inside and out examination concerning these ethology concentrates could empower an increasingly receptive frame of mind towards dog behavior. Then, methods based on etiology can never furnish clear enough rules even with the guide of "dog-whisperer" high achievers like Jan Fennell and Cesar Millan.

"The Art of Effective Dog Training" is an excellent example of an expert dog training course that you can show you the correct techniques to accurately prepare your dog to carry on appropriately regularly. This fundamental training unit is additionally compact and contains concentrates based on individual circumstances — the methods here based on techniques educated by expert dog trainers. If you sign up now, you will likewise approach great free online discussions. Without a doubt by rehearsing the simple to-pursue well-ordered rules clarified in the specialty of practical dog training, steadily and with consistency your dog will come to remember you as the alpha dog in the blink of an eye.

CHAPTER THREE
Great Dog Training Techniques

A dog gives unrestricted love and companionship to a minding proprietor. A well-trained dog expands your pleasure and fulfillment ten times over when contrasted with an untrained dog. Studies have demonstrated that a well-trained dog is a more joyful and more substance creature than one who isn't. I have effective in achieving this with positively no mercilessness and without breaking a dog's soul. When legitimate training techniques are utilized, you will be astonished how rapidly a dog will figure out how to pursue your commands. Coming up next are instances of some incredible dog training techniques you can use to show your dog some fundamental compliance abilities:

The Sit Command -

This is the most well-known and fundamental command to show your dog and presumably ought to be the main thing you educate him. Utilizing a treat as a reward for ethical conduct functions admirably for generally training. You will require a chain joined to your dog's restraint to hold him unfaltering. Demonstrate your dog a treat that you have in your hand. Sometimes, just by pressing the treat over his head, your dog will consequently sit. If he doesn't lie, place your other hand on your dog's back and gently press down, saying, "Sit." When he sits, reward him promptly with the treat and recognition him by saying "Well-done Boy" in a delightful tone and pet him vigorously showing him you are satisfied with his reaction to your "Sit" command. It's imperative to reward him following he reacts effectively, so he knows why he is accepting the reward.

The Lie Down Command -

When your dog has aced the sit command, you can advance to the "Rests" command. A treat is additionally used to achieve this. The first request that your dog "Sit." Try not to give him a gift for sitting. When he is in the sitting position, you ought to have a treat in your hand and hold it before him, exceptionally near the floor and state "Rests." If first spot your other hand on your dog's shoulders and gently press down until your dog lies down or give him a delicate pull descending on his chain. When your dog lies down, reward him quickly with a treat and state "Good Boy" in a delightful tone and pet him vigorously showing him you are satisfied with his reaction to your "Rests" command. The tone of your voice is imperative to let your pet realize you are happy with his response to your command.

Stay Command -

The "Remain" command is somewhat more testing than the Sit and Lie Down Commands. It is critical to pick a suitable time during the day to begin working with your dog on the "Remain" command. Knowing your very own dog and perceiving when he is showing a loose or smooth personality is significant. You would prefer not to begin this training when your dog is energized or excessively lively. Likewise, with the past training commands, it is valuable to utilize a treat when instructing the "Remain" command. To begin this, training gives your dog the sit or rests authority. When he is eating or sitting "Remain" and hold your hand up as though you were flagging somebody to stop. Wythe dog does not move for 4 or 5 seconds, give him a treat and state "Good Boy" and pet him. Possibly provide him with acclaim if he remains for the 4 or 5 seconds. If he doesn't comply with your command, attempt once. You may need to rehash the "Remain" command a couple of times and put your hand in a stop position to urge him to remain. As he begins to comprehend, give him the "Remain" command and gradually step back a couple of feet, continuously expanding the separation until he expects the "Remain" command. Keep it, and it is essential to be persistent with your dog when training if training isn't practical today, attempt again on one more day. Tolerance and industriousness are continuously rewarded.

Utilize Traditional Training Techniques -

When I talk about "Customary" training techniques, I am alluding to a couple of essential techniques that are significant in training your dog.

- The first and most significant is tolerance. You should be tolerant of your dog when showing him new things. Similarly, as with individuals, different dogs learn at different paces. If your dog isn't getting on to another command, be tolerant! Try not to holler or menace your dog. Sometimes it's smarter to quit training and begin once more day again.

- Voice articulation is another significant piece of training your dog. I allude to this as talking in a "Happy Voice" to reward your dog when he reacts to your command effectively.

- Using dog treats is another usual or customary method for training your dog. Although gifts are helpful in the underlying training of a command, you would prefer not to need to convey a pocket brimming with treats with you consistently all together for your dog to comply with your authorities. You have to bit by bit kill the gifts once your dog has aced another command and supplant it with a "Good Boy" and hot petting.

- Significantly, everybody in your family utilizes precisely the same commands, so your dog does not end up confounded on what is being asked of him, for example, "rests" versus "down." It doesn't make a difference what the command is, the length of everybody is utilizing a similar control.

- Finally, you have to make your training sessions a good time for your dog. He should connect a training session by having a fabulous time. Thus, after a training session, you should play with your dog for ten or fifteen minutes, making the session pleasant for both you and your dog.

Having a well-trained dog is one of life's delights.

USE THESE PUPPY TRAINING TECHNIQUES
FOR BETTER SUCCESS

Puppy training techniques are essential assets in raising a puppy. Teaching a puppy, the skills necessary for socialization and obedience can help calm the dissatisfactions that accompany having an untrained puppy. Not all young doggies are similarly responsive to training, nonetheless, and finding the strategies that best fit the puppy's needs will guarantee the best result.

Training a puppy requires time and commitment from the owner or coach. A few young doggies might be usually disposed towards forceful or hostile to social conduct. In such cases, persistence is vital, and the owner must keep on fortifying the training regardless of whether the puppy commits rehashed errors. A significant point to consider in dog training is the creature's age. While conduct issues in completely developed dogs can be revised with the correct techniques, it is commonly a lot simpler to prepare another puppy or a more youthful dog. If conceivable start training the puppy at 6 two months. The puppy's age frequently figures out which training strategies are the most reasonable.

The initial phase in training is to familiarize the dog with its new home and environment. House training includes such puppy training techniques as case training, potty training, and acknowledgment of straightforward commands. The capacity of the puppy to perceive such powers as "sit," "come," and "remain" are particularly significant. These directions fill in as a reason for future training and guarantee the wellbeing of the puppy in an open setting.

Socialization is another significant part of puppy training. If appropriately mingled, the dog will almost certainly interface with different people and creatures without returning to terrified or forceful conduct. Else, it might be essential to sequester the dog to its home consistently to forestall mischief to itself and other people. The initial three months of a dog's life is necessary for teaching socialization skills; after the initial 12 weeks, it is critical to fortify and refine these skills.

Leash training and obedience training are fundamental in teaching a puppy to be polite. Training a puppy to stroll on a leash is twofold: the puppy should initially be fitted with a neckline, and after that, it winds up familiar with a rope. The neckline ought to be a cozy fit; however, without being prohibitively so. Leash training enables the owner to walk the puppy securely in an outside setting. Obedience training shows the puppy to react to a command and keeps the puppy from taking part in ruinous conduct.

A couple of straightforward tips can improve the achievement pace of most puppy training techniques. Training a puppy requires encouraging feedback. Reward the puppy with commendation or seasonal treats when it effectively pursues a command. Uplifting feedback will assist the puppy with bettering retain the training. Beginning training in an area that is free from diversions will facilitate the procedure for both the dog and its owner.

How to Communicate Using Dog Training Hand Signals

Training dogs can be useful with hand signals. This is a decent decision for you to turn into an ace the craft of practical dog training

puppy training gestures or positive hand signals are used for commanding your canine to execute an assortment of commands. Albeit numerous canine proprietors train dogs by executing worded commands, different proprietors pick a blend of all worded commands and dog training hand gestures. These proprietors appreciate many points of interest in training their dogs this way. Without a doubt, dogs ordinarily use visual signals to talk. Your canine may usually grasp physical gestures superior to worded commands.

Hand gestures, in fact, function admirably in models where worded commands don't fill in also. One case is the place worded commands can't be recognized in episodes of stiff breeze or from an extraordinary separation, anyway hand signals can regularly be seen, and canines that experience difficulty hearing will enormously profit in this regard.

Some dog proprietors overlook worded commands completely and use canine training hand gestures without anyone else's input. Point of fact, seeing a canine reply to hand signals alone is sufficient and is a decent begin to rehearsing your useful dog training abilities.

Motivations to pick hand gestures over verbal commands

With practical dog training, there are some valid justifications for utilizing dog training hand gestures are as per the following - dogs can see body language as an approach to converse with one another. In a lot of ways, it very well may be simpler for your canine to comprehend hand gestures than worded commands.

Likewise, if your canine is out of hearing separation, it might most likely pick the hand gesture. This the way that trainers who train chasing dogs or dexterity canines figure out how to hold their canine's conduct under administration. In these occasions, the chasing canine is commonly far away. If it is encouraged to hand signals, the controller at that point can tell his canine what sort of technique of activity it is.

In the case that your canine flees, if you are rehearsing effective dog training techniques that require skill, or chasing, your canine may not comply with your worded commands, however, may notice well the signal you make with your hand.

Usually, in specific situations where there is a canine who can't hear appropriately, at that point, using this strategy empowers you to train without having state any verbal command.

When a dog is energized, it may not listen fabulously, yet there is a higher possibility that it will reply to what it can see before him. Unavoidably, if a dog can know that it needs to focus on you for a command, it will hold its concentration and can be simpler to train.

By and large, the best thought is to utilize the two sorts of commands in a consolidated manner, as dog training hand signals support worded commands. In the remote possibility that you use hand signals with these voice commands, you will likewise appreciate some distinct useful dog training points of interest.

Notwithstanding those referenced above, for example, being active at more noteworthy separations and being reasonable for canines with debilitated hearing, such preferences include:

Your canine is in all probability going to watch you when it understands that it needs to see your commands to satisfy them. It is conceivable that your canine could endeavor to disregard a verbal command, yet it likely won't overlook your hand signal.

The fundamental dog training hand gesture

A dog that is energized will reply preferred to hand signals over spoken commands.

Command to sit

Begin with your arm brought down, alongside your body, and with your fingers indicated down the ground. Bring your hand and forearm up, and twist your arm at the elbow.

When this development is done, your palm should face up with your hand, which ought to be over your dog's head. In the remote possibility that you have a treat in your hand, your canine will finish the gesture hand with his eyes and nose. His base will presumably bring down with the end goal for him to wind up sitting.

Regardless of some canine proprietors having built up their own specific dog training hand signals, the vast majority of them feel that on a pretty much arrangement of hand signals, that are utilized for fundamental submission commands. Here are a few instances of some essential, however effective dog training techniques using hand signals.

Command to remain

Start by bringing your canine into a situated or downwards pose. Move your hand, so you are holding it at your arm's length before your canine's face, as in the remote possibility that you were a police officer commanding him to stop. Your palm should confront his nose, so your fingers are pointed upwards.

The downwards command

Start with your arm outstretched before you and your palm downwards confronted. Drop your weapon until it stops against your side together with your fingers pointed straight down.

Command to heel

This strategy trains your canine to shift to one side, so your left thigh is tapped with your left hand. Should your canine be before you, teach him to position himself by driving him behind you, from the side on you towards the party to your left hand?

Command to come

Give your left arm a chance to be straight before your body and hold it there. At that point, move your hand over your body so your left hand, in the long run, contacts your correct shoulder. Rush the movement of your arm when your canine learns the command.

When you are accustomed to actualizing hand gestures, do remember the verbal privilege command simultaneously, you are giving the hand signal. These will ensure that both are fortified, and the impact of your active dog training will be reinforced. You should likewise remember consistency, regardless of whether you are giving a verbal or physical command. Regardless of a modest development, this may cause your canine to accept that you're empowering them some elective commandment.

Should you use similar signals without fail, your dog will, in the end, agree.

Worded commands are useful, yet they not in every case inherently capable of being heard except if your dog is close-by. A hand gesture is that as it may, as it tends to be seen from a separation, may well spare your canine's life and keep him from running into traffic, particularly when joined with worded commands.

Also, you can get familiar with effective dog training techniques. There are seminars on practical dog training on the web where you will be given careful instruction in training your dog and the best in consolidating hand signals with verbal commands.

The Art of Effective Dog Training is one such course that can enable you to turn into a moment effective trainer of your own. By rehearsing the unmistakably clarified well-ordered directions in this compact dog training course with the faithful perseverance and ingenuity, you also can turn into the pleased proprietor of a polite, loyal dog.

Electronic Dog Training

When individuals become acquainted with electronic training items and use them appropriately, they discover the philosophy is demonstrated, proficient, prudent, and moral.

The kind of training where an electronic guide is utilized is essential, for it will impact the sort of item and techniques used. Is the equipment being used to encourage another obedience command, right some basic misbehavior, or is it being utilized to strengthen another electronic training philosophy?

Components influencing accomplishment Before an electronic training instrument is utilized, it is firmly proposed that the whole training situation be reevaluated. There are three unique contemplations in this re-assessment:

The owner does know what he is doing? Does he comprehend the training procedure, and would he be able to apply the appropriate system to a specific situation?

Is the owner training the dog appropriately, does he have an arrangement for this specific misbehavior, and will he say he is executing that arrangement suitably and accurately?

Is the dog trainable? Is the dog being referred to stressful, stuck in a rut, or unintelligent?

(We accept that all dogs are trainable. Dogs that appear to be obstinate, or unintelligent, have not been prepared appropriately, reliably, or effectively.)

Of these elements, the initial two are generally necessary. If training isn't fruitful, much of the time it is because owner instruction, readiness, consistency or responsibility is deficient. This might be difficult for individual owners to acknowledge, however, recollect that we have welcomed dogs into our condition. It is our way to train them in manners they can get it. This is fantastically important, in such a case that an owner has not taken the time, or connected the fitting techniques appropriately and reliably, training with an electronic item won't have any effect. It will just befuddle even the most astute dog.

There is the sure flag that proposes a dog has not been appropriately prepared. In these occurrences a dog may:

Oppose when his owner endeavors to put a collar around his neck.

Withstand correction, of any sort, within sight of specific diversions

Control his owner by acting bashful or by disregarding his owner

Frenzy when he detects a notice.

Endeavor to escape when accepting a correction

Do anything aside from the behavior essential to stay away from the correction.

Training is the key. If an owner sets aside the effort to comprehend electronic training - why it works, how it works, how to apply the suitable techniques - it very well may be a helpful instrument.

Electronic training requires information and expertise. Why worry about appropriate instruction? In light of the most significant variable in the condition - the owner. Give us a chance to confront it, people are genuinely erratic, to the extent dogs are concerned. The reaction of most owners to the requirement for correction fluctuates broadly, contingent upon the dog, the training, the current situation, and even the state of mind they happen to be in at the time. This isn't helpful for practical training - of any sort.

As a rule, a dog shows behavior in light of some upgrade or diversion. Owners must be mindful so as not to make one more, different misconduct by mis-applying the applying or correction it at the wrong time. Furthermore, for the security of the dog, it is pointless to address it for each seemingly insignificant detail. Owners must be specific to keep away from canine perplexity. When connected appropriately, electronic training should be possible effectively. To help get this, let us inspect how individuals react to their dog without electronics.

Dog owners react to their puppy in any number of different ways. They may reward their dog by petting, talking, providing food or treats, playing, or giving them a chance to rest on the bed. The rundown is insofar as there are owners on it. These equivalent owners likewise right in different ways, including hollering, hitting, tossing things, the utilization of a steel training collar, disregarding their dog, not providing food or treats, or seclusion in a room, box, or pet hotel. This does not infer that these types of reward and correction are satisfactory. Just that they are various, and that training can be fruitful under a portion of these conditions. So it is with electronic training.

One of the best-recognized points of interest in electronic training is that modern electronics do make us people progressively unsurprising. It upgrades human consistency, particularly as it identifies with correction. It additionally enables people to productively and helpfully apply suitable corrections, notwithstanding when a dog isn't inside the scope of customary (chain and choker collar) correction techniques.

Rules of electronic training As was referenced before, electronic training works on a similar fundamental standard utilized in all canine behavior modification: correction, redirection, and reward. In this manner, the dog must comprehend the rudiments before progressively complex training starts.

'Dummy Equipment Effect': Before electronic dog training starts, the owner/trainer should be agreeable in the utilization of the gadget, and the dog should be pleasant, too. Accordingly, it is essential to make the 'Dummy Equipment Effect' before starting.

Dogs are exceptionally canny and brilliant enough to know the difference between the different sorts of collars being utilized. They appear to be unique. They smell different. They apply different weights on the neck once they are connected. Indeed, even the owner/trainer acts differently with the different collars. Now and again, the owner/trainer is there; in various cases, he isn't.

Since the majority of this is valid, it is essential to dispose of the equipment itself from the learning procedure. Here is the secret.

Before starting to prepare with a functioning electronic collar, the dog should initially wind up acquainted with a deactivated collar (i.e., take the battery out). Regardless of whether the dog trainer or dog owner is experiencing strain to prepare the dog rapidly (e.g., the neighbors are grumbling), despite everything he needs to show the dog that the collar isn't something to be dreaded.

General Rules: All of the general rules of obedience training apply to electronic practice also. They are most likely considerably progressively important in electronic training. These rules include:

Try not to prepare the dog for expanded timeframes.

Point of confinement the quantity of corrections the dog gets in a single training session and one training day.

Make sure that corrections are appropriately offset with reward.

Continuously give the correction simultaneously. That is; do such just when the dog is making trouble, not before the misbehavior happens or after the transgression has ceased. This is significant because it allows the dog to learn (i.e., to comprehend what causes the correction in any way).

In the end, the starting purpose of most electronic training incorporates the utilization of a chain, which serves to help divert the dog away from the break and other unseemly reactions. This, thus, makes it progressively important not to address self-assertively or out of disappointment. As a puppy trainer or owner, it is essential to be as restrained as you need the dog to be.

The significance of redirection and reward Electronic training joins a few different techniques. Applying a correction is just a little piece of a training program. Redirection and recognition are unmistakably progressively significant.

Why is this philosophy critical? Assume there is a dog in a regulatory framework. What ought to be the ideal correction? He should come when he is called, remain in the yard, and quit yelping at the jogger. In any case, pursuing and yapping are impeccably ordinary in a dog's typical habitat. Just in the human condition, are they wrong?

Accordingly, if the owner/trainer truly needs to prepare the dog under these conditions, he should initially address at a suitable time, and reliably. He would do as such, utilizing an obedience command. Along these lines, before starting increasingly confounded electronic training, the dog must comprehend fundamental obedience commands. The trainer/owner must form from a strong establishment given by these training essentials.

In this specific occurrence, when the puppy is running, he would be taken the 'Come' command. Not because he is pursuing a jogger. On the other hand, when the dog obeys quickly, he is adulated for reacting to the power, not for severing his interest. This is called redirection.

The dangers of electronic training are numerous factors. This similar situation took care of inappropriately, can have the contrary effect. It could prepare the dog to assault joggers. A correction at the wrong time may make the dog identify the correction boost with the jogger. Dogs are known to have battle or flight reactions to such dangers. If the dog's response is to 'battle,' joggers be careful!

Advantage: Unfortunately, some dog trainers/owners put the accentuation on the correction. Indeed, even in this chapter, the data is weighted around there. This is because the correction is where most training issues happen. The reward is a lot of more straightforward idea to comprehend and apply. During training, the dog ought to continually and reliably be given a merited reward - ideally recognition and petting - for behavior that meets his training targets. Once more, timing is essential. The dog must almost certainly make the association between the reward and the appropriate action.

A needless reward is likewise a no-no. The dog trainer must reward the dog just when he is carrying on appropriately. Try not to stress, and there will be a lot of chances to do as such. Except if, obviously, the dog trainer/owner pants off and rewards conflictingly; or he separates further and treats the do.

An unwarranted reward is additionally a no-no. The dog trainer must reward the dog just when he is acting appropriately. Try not to stress, and there will be a lot of chances to do as such. Except if, obviously, the dog trainer/owner pants off and rewards conflictingly; or he separates further and gets the dog applause, petting, and food, regardless of whether a behavior is improper.

Enthusiastic and vitality outlet: Appropriate passionate outlets additionally bear some talk in this specific circumstance. Electronic training is intended to prevent a dog from displaying misbehaviors, and help reward him for what the dog trainer/owner thinks about proper behavior. Be that as it may, if a dog can't leave the yard, no reward can supplant the opportunity he has lost. In such cases, a puppy must be given other fitting outlets. This is why exercises, like running with the dog or playing with him, are critical.

Redirection: Redirection is similarly essential, if not more so. In numerous electronic training situations, the dog trainer/owner needs to give a substitute behavior to the dog. This redirection provides a realized behavior pattern that the dog can fall back on, empowering the dog trainer/owner to reward him. A genuine case of such a behavior pattern is the 'Sit,' 'Take care of business your ball,' or other command the dog as of now gets it.

Have an arrangement: Overall, what one attempts to do with redirection and reward is assemble better behavior in the dog. In any case, when building anything, it is helpful to have a diagram - an arrangement that frameworks individually what to do under a variety of conditions.

As a result of the considerable number of factors associated with electronic training, the dog trainer/owner needs such an arrangement. He has to know precisely what he will do before a situation emerges. Since, when it comes to training dogs, he needs to expect the unforeseen. Be that as it may, if there is an arrangement set up, he will know precisely what to do.

Aggressive Dog Training Made Easy

Dog aggression is a genuine underlying problem that numerous proprietors will look at one time in their dog's life or another. There must be tons of studies related to aggression. Questions, for example, "Why does aggression happen," "Why are a few breeds progressively forceful," and "How might I utilize forceful dog training to control aggression in my dog," are asked all the time. Before you start practical dog training, it is essential to comprehend the type of aggression that your dog might involvement. In all honesty, there are a few types of attack, and everyone should be handled in a marginally different manner. The types of aggression are:

- **Dog Aggression:** this can be seen in various breeds, and it is aggression that a dog shows to different dogs. · Fear Aggression: Many people may not consider fear to be a dynamic behavior but rather if a dog starts to chew, bark, snarl or kick up some dust when he is scared than it has moved from straightforward fear to fear aggression.

- **Dominant Aggression:** This is an intense type of aggression since the dog has numerous attributes that you would find in a "domineering jerk." One of the most severe issues with an overwhelming attack is that it isn't generally observed as aggression, only an alpha character doing what it specializes in until the dog assaults a person or thing. Another problem is that prevailing aggression is entirely unusual.

- **Possessive Aggression**: To get a reasonable thought of this, watch your dog while he is eating and is hindered by somebody. If he snarls or chomps then you realize that he is possessive about things he saves as his. While this may appear to be suitable, a dog should never be possessive.

- **Pain Aggression:** This is aggression that is demonstrated when a dog is in pain. · Maternal Aggression: Seen distinctly in female dogs, this is an aggression that is seen when a female is raising a litter of pups.

- **Learn Aggression:** There are a few types of dogs that are inclined to regional aggression where they see a region, for example, the house, the yard, the area or the majority of the above as his. When different creatures or people enter his domain, he responds emphatically.

As should be obvious, there is an enormous number of aggressions, and numerous dogs will encounter either at specific times in their life. While a few types of aggression are intense and require practical dog training, some of them aren't and incredibly require some tolerance by the proprietor to survive. On account of pain aggression, it is critical to discover why your dog is forceful. If he is harmed, take him to the vet to have the problem taken care of. When the dog mends, the aggression ought to leave without anyone else; however, if it doesn't, you can move into training strategies for it.

What's more, maternal aggression can be kept away from essentially by fixing your dog yet if she whelps a litter, the maternal aggression ought to lessen as the doggies are weaned and placed in new homes. By and large, the most straightforward approach to utilize practical dog training is to mingle your puppy and dog accurately. Numerous people consider socialization to be a procedure that is done when their puppy is youthful; however, socialization ought to be done all through your dog's life. Presenting him to different dogs, people, places, and stimulants will help control a wide range of regions of aggression, for example, dog aggression. never forget that when you do mingle your dog, particularly if he has some aggression problems, that you do as such in a controlled manner.

Ensure every one of the dogs is on chains and acquaint him with one dog at a time. Never enable your dog to be encompassed by a gathering of dogs since this can scare him and trigger his forceful reaction. If whenever your dog begins to demonstrate aggression, basically right him by evacuating him a couple of feet from the other dog and after that lauding him when he quiets down. Another approach to make forceful dog training simple is to place firm guidelines in your home from the minute your dog arrives home. This implies he isn't permitted on the furnishings and that he comprehends that the house is yours. To fight strength aggression, it is critical to put yourself and every other person in the job of the rule. Your dog ought to never eat the family, and he ought to never be permitted to discover nourishment for himself.

When he eats, set aside the effort to place your hands in the dog's sustenance dish and feed him by hand. This instructs him that anybody is permitted in his meal, and it will help control some possessive aggression. Ensure that everybody in the house does this also and never let the dog circumvent your hand to eat straightforwardly from the bowl. As a rule, practical dog training needs to begin with proprietors. To make it simple, you have to take a gander at how you are training your dog, how he is being mingled, and what negative behaviors are being strengthened. For example, if you sustain trepidation reactions, for instance, snarling by indulging the dog whenever he is terrified, at that point, he will rapidly discover that snarling is the best possible reaction to being frightened, which may form into fear aggression.

Disregard a few behaviors and right others with a firm "no," which is a significant direction with practical dog training. When you are utilizing effective dog training, you mustn't right your dog in a brutal manner. Even though it may not appear as though you are harsh to your dog, a little slap can cause a lot of harm, and if a dog is as of now forceful, it will merely strengthen the dynamic behavior. After you have amended how you train your dog, the time has come to begin practical dog training, and it is simple; permanently break out the nuts and bolts of the practice. Commonly, fundamental training all the time can truly help with numerous types of aggression and a wide range of kinds of negative behaviors.

To fight regional aggression, begin by welcoming people once again to your home and remedying your dog when he starts yelping with a loud commotion to intrude on the behavior and after that a firm "no." When your dog quits woofing, acclaim him and treat. Increment the recurrence that different visitors visit as your dog winds up familiar with people being in his space. If your dog is forceful during strolls, the time has come to take vigorous dog training out on a walk. Begin by taking different courses each time you go for a stroll. Since the course is different, your dog is more reluctant to engrave a path similar to his.

When he meets people or different creatures in the city, right his contrary behavior with a firm "no" and acclaim him when he doesn't respond. As practical dog training is progressed, bit by bit starts taking him to higher traffic territories until he can stroll in a bustling place without meeting energetically. Albeit practical dog training is genuinely straightforward, it takes some time, and it is critical to watch your dog's feelings of anxiety and to take as much time as is needed with training. Keep in mind, your dog didn't end up forceful overnight, and you can't expect the practical dog training to work medium-term either, so take as much time as is needed and appreciate each achievement your dog has.

CHAPTER FOUR
Dog Training Tools and Advice

In the first place, let us get rid of the fantasy that your dog's seem to give in on a mindset as a creature; they do not. I realize this is difficult to take, and we as a whole love to accept that our great kid is quite keen. The fact of the matter is the dog will talk to you. You need to instruct yourself to train your dog. Individuals regularly commit gigantic unexpected errors concerning training dogs, absolutely because they don't comprehend the dog's mind. Your dog requires certain vital factors to be accurately trained, and you need to realize how to do this. Fundamentally you need to arm yourself with the best dog training tools accessible in the market today. This may contain physical gadgets alongside reliable training advice. Your dog just truly needs to be a faithful individual from his dog pack. Dogs carry on intuitively, being a creature; this is very typical. All they need is acknowledgment. To change any lousy dog behavior, you need to concentrate on improving how your dog communicates his regular dog impulses. Shouting and being furious with your dog won't train the dog. This will make absence and dread of certainty inside your dog.

Center Dog Training Advice

There are numerous regions wherein one could train your dog. A portion of these territories is only for recreational exercises. For example, you may need your dog to do stunts like rollover or give paw, and so on. These are only for gloating rights; indeed, perceive how smart my dog is. In this, there is an increasingly positive side to training. Here you would need some further developed dog training tools or advice. This sort of training includes keeping up control of your dog when out in broad daylight or your own home when abnormal individuals are visiting, for example. Paradise comprehends what a badly-behaved dog can get up to if not held within proper limits. Bad dog behavior can cost their proprietors beyond all doubt, so it is prudent to concentrate on these parts of dog training. Here are a couple of the nuts and bolts concerning dog training; As we realize this is a significant tremendous subject, so we will cover some increasingly outstanding dog behavior problem. There is a lot to pay for, and worth each penny, proficient instructional aides out there. Let us investigate a portion of these lousy dog behavior issues which require training of your dog, presently.

Crate Training:

This kind of dog training device ought not to be manhandled, for instance, when you need to a break from your pet dog. Crate training ought to be utilized to appropriately house train your dog. You may likewise need to acclimate your dog with the crate for that event when he would go with you on a plane, for example. The thought is to limit the dog to the container for a brief timeframe, lets state 60 minutes. Upon discharge from the crate, you should take the dog outside to enable him to do his business. If the puppy does his business, then a reward as a reliable dog treat or pampering them with love is altogether. Indeed, we see here excellent behavior related to remuneration. Quick pointers here, consistently be at home when utilizing the crate, don't secure the dog in the container medium-term, ensure the dog is agreeable in the bottle. Never enable the container to be viewed as a type of discipline for your dog. Dogs respond intuitively and all things considered, ought not to be beaten or yelled at doing what falls into place without a hitch.

Leash Training:

If your dog is hauling your arm out of its attachment each time you take him walkies, it's time for appropriate leash training; You need to assume control of your dog when he is on the leash. If important cause your dog to sit and remain while you proceed to open the entryway. At that point return, put on his leash, just if he has behaved and tuned in to your commands. Redundancy is critical here if you need to be freed of his over passionate behavior. Likewise, as long as your dog is in this advertised upstate, he won't tune in to any commands you may give him. While strolling your dog, you ought to consistently be in charge. The dog ought not to be driving you around. By all methods, let the dog sniff about, etc., however, not all through the entire walk.

The Alpha Position:

Each tamed dog needs to be trained around there. In no way, shape or form should your dog be permitted to assume this job in your home or outside so far as that is concerned. Dogs don't talk, they bark, except the Basenji type obviously, so don't assume dogs comprehend human language. At last, your dog needs to realize that you are in control and accordingly, your dog can unwind, realizing that you will secure him. I know this sounds weird; the same number of us assume the dog is there to defend us. Make no blunder; your dog will unquestionably "go to the gathering" when his pack or any of its individuals is under danger. This serves to re-uphold the idea of setting up the pack jobs with the goal that your dog knows precisely who is in and who isn't.

Compliance Training:

Presently I don't think about you, yet I unquestionably was not brought into the world a specialist in dog training. So here, I would state it's fitting to attempt to go to some excellent dutifulness training classes. This is particularly valid if you are another dog proprietor or have never honestly had any expert advice from individuals that have been doing this once a day. All that you are educated at these classes can be utilized in your home training. These classes can give a strong establishment to angles, for example, expecting the alpha position, house training, issuing commands and notwithstanding dealing with your more seasoned increasingly adult dogs. When you have the rudiments, there is an abundance of advice, items, and information out there from specialists in their fields, which will engage you. It might cost a bit. However, I would prefer to be unable to balance a checkbook.

Dog Training Advice - Consistency is essential.

Dogs learn things by methods for reiteration, and this has been settled as of now. Thus, for you to have any accomplishment in controlling your dog or dogs, you need to be CONSISTENT. Indeed, this is genuinely the one most significant thing when it comes to dog training. No matter how you live alone or have a gigantic family at home, dog training is fundamental to keep up harmony and amicability, don't bother the bank balance. This is basic if you have a family or offer your home with other individuals. You should teach the family or other individuals also, with the goal that the dog sees a CONSISTENT hierarchy of leadership. Sounds military. However, I guess this frame of mind is required if you need to take out bad dog behavior. There is no reason for you investing all the push to get your dog trained and respectful, only for the remainder of the family to proceed to demolish everything. This will truly make your dog befuddled too.

Continuously recollect that any learning increased through classes, a quality online book you have purchased or by merely perusing these books, is going to profit you eventually. KNOWLEDGE is POWER, and that is so valid. Your dog might be physically more dominant than you. However, you are overwhelming in light of KNOWLEDGE.

Dog Training - Three Stages of Dog Training

Three stages of puppy training, and, significantly, you get them if you are going to prepare your dog appropriately adequately. When you see everyone, you will probably identify your dog's advancement and use this to hone numerous parts of your dog's training.

If you are keen on teaching stunts or doggy moving, at that point, you must figure out how to perceive these different phases. You will find that your dog will advance at different stages for various practices. As you shape your dog's reactions, you should remember what stage your dog is up to in its advancement.

If you needed to show your dog to drop, move over, play dead and after that jump back up once more. You would need to do this in sections. It is difficult to show it as one movement. Your dog should initially figure out how to drop, at that point move over - the whole distance, at that point lay its head down and afterward it would need to discover that it could not get up until you gave it a discharge command. This can be accomplished by binding the different activities together. As you started teaching each stage independently, you should know about the different phases your dog is up to in its learning.

The main stage is the teaching phase. At this stage, we are teaching or demonstrating the dog what it is that we need the person in question to do. We use rewards as well as treats after each fruitful endeavor during this stage, and we should be incredibly understanding.

The teaching phase includes you demonstrating your dog what it is that you need. This may consist of taking care of your puppy and utilizing baiting to get your dog into a position that you need.

When we were teaching sit, we hold a treat directly before the dog's nose and afterward move it backward. The dog will typically move into a sit position;

then you will reward and discharge. If the dog doesn't move into the area that you need, it doesn't get the treat. As you place the gift before the dog's nose, give the command 'sit' also. When your dog will necessarily 'sit' without you attracting it into position, it has moved from the teaching to the training phase. This will happen practically overnight with most little dogs; however, different commands may take weeks if not months to prepare.

It is essential in social training to recall the teaching phase, as well. For instance, a few dogs and most pups can't support themselves and need to jump all over you. If your dog is figuring out how to 'sit' and is in the teaching phase, you can't hope to have the option to divert it and reward for sitting. You may need to hold your puppy in a sit or 'four on the floor' position, as I call it, and after that you give gift. You can do this by putting your thumb in its neckline and holding it down.

When your puppy has learned not to jump on you but instead wait in a sit for a pat and the consideration it pines for, it is in the training phase.

The subsequent stage is the training phase.

At the training phase, we can start to hone your dog's reaction time and how they react. At this stage, you should be fulfilled that your dog knows the command, both verbal and hand signals.

You ought to likewise be utilizing treats discontinuously during this stage also planning to wean your dog off them.

If your dog realizes how to sit; however, it kicks it legs out to the side or isn't loose, right now is an ideal opportunity to start to hone up this conduct. How? It's simple. When you request that your dog sit and it doesn't do it how you might want don't reward. State 'no'; make a stride back and after that re-command 'sit.' I generally return a step to give my dogs a chance and the space to address their conduct.

There is no compelling reason to use unforgiving amendments or to begin hollering at your dog. I have all around prepared dogs that hang off my every word. I have never hit them. I don't reward for conduct I don't need.

When you were confident that your dog has finished the training stage, it's time for you to move the person in question onto the proofing stage. This is the third stage.

There is the same number of different times and places to get your dog through to the proofing stage. Your creative mind constrains them. Proofing your dog implies that your dog will play out anything you have prepared it to do anyplace. A few places that ring a bell our kids' play area, schools, dog stops, shops or close homestead creatures or animals. Ensure that you have your dog on a rope and have control of it to abstain from stumbling into hardship.

A great many people wrongly take their dog out in open sometime before it is prepared. Without a doubt, it can perform convoluted assignments at home; however, in the recreation center with such a large number of different sights and scents? I don't think so.

While I acquaint essential acquiescence commands with my puppy classes, I state, again and again, and this is the awful condition to start teaching your puppy because there are very numerous distractions. Who needs to figure out how to sit when there is a room loaded with different doggies and individuals to sniff, lick, move around with and unleash ruin with? No healthy puppy, I know! So, while I show the how's and whys, I tell my customers that they should start to rehearse these commands at home where it is calm, and there are not many distractions.

When proofing your dog recollect that you should make a couple of strides backward in its training. Try not to anticipate excessively and consistently, consistently reward for exertion. If you start to lose your temper and you give off an impression of being pestering your dog to accomplish something it doesn't comprehend your dog will close down and won't hear you out by any stretch of the imagination.

You may likewise need to expand your dog's inspiration when proofing it. This implies you may need to use beautiful treats, for example, cheddar or kabana, be significantly more excited with your voice and give exceptionally liberal sincere taps. You will be facing a great deal of exceptionally fascinating distractions so you should arm yourself properly!

Continuously be patient and make sure to reward what you need; wait quietly for what you might want from your dog and don't use power or discipline.

This will enable you to assemble a substantially more important association with your dog dependent on trust and regard.

Positive and Negative Reinforcement Dog Training - What Works?

It is essential to point out to ourselves that dogs are of a different animal variety than ourselves, and accordingly, our assumptions may not fulfill the way they act. In the least complex terms, you can consider dogs learning by utilizing experimentation; that is, they will carry on in a wide scope of different methodologies and dependent on the consequences of those behaviors/actions, they will either increment or decline the recurrence of those behaviors. Know it or not, your dog is adapting persistently by focusing on its encompassing and the consequences of its actions and social interactions. Your dog (in specific cases, like us), will attempt to keep away from behavior that outcomes in negative consequences or whatever that causes the enormous results to vanish.

Keep in mind your German Shepherd is one of the most gifted dogs, and it's protected to state that you and your dog will have a more beneficial relationship whenever your dog considers you to be a facilitator to enormous consequences. Consider it, your dog's happiness genuinely hinges on you as the owner. From the opportunity to associate with different dogs at parks, going for strolls about the area, or notwithstanding having a delectable dinner, you have the choosing key! Subsequently, if you do uncover these open doors for your dog to profit by positive encounters, your dog will more be slanted than not to work with you.

This truly is the way of thinking behind the way toward compensating your dog for right actions and is viewed as uplifting feedback training. The wide assortment of choices you can do to empower excellent behavior are varied and comprise of nearly anything from treats just as new toys to appreciating additional time in the dog stops or petting your dog. Encouraging feedback training more often than not functions admirably given that all together for your dog to understand things that he acknowledges/appreciates, he should acquire them by collaborating with you. Uplifting feedback training centers around the "dos" as opposed to the "don'ts."

Now, you're in all probability pondering: What about discipline or what is otherwise called negative reinforcement? Many dog coaches would agree that punishing your dog for something that he/she did is never going to enable your dog to make a move in a progressively excellent or proper way. Also, rebuffing your dog is HARMFUL! Notwithstanding that, it can likewise strain the bond both of you share, which as we have delineated, can make training your dog impressively more disappointing than it should be. Another bothersome impact of negative reinforcement is that your dog will start communicating behaviors of accommodation and dread you anytime - the punisher - are available. What's more, when you're absent, your dog will return to carrying on a similar way he/she was restrained for. Attempt to recall a time when you were close to nothing, and your folks educated you "no" to specific exercises; what did you turn out doing?

The youthful me, for one, wouldn't have given in without difficulty. Instead, I most likely would have continued bothering my folks for the things I looked for. I bring this up because I accept like a large number of us can partner to such situations and hence acknowledge why negative reinforcement training doesn't (generally) take care of business. From related involvements, I have seen individuals rebuffing (how about we not broadly expound how) their dogs for delving holes in their home yard which just brought about more hole diving if there is nobody present at home. Let's face it, once in a while, and dog owners would feel so debilitated with the actions of their dogs that they have the air to act out of their intuition and rebuff their dogs. It ought to be emphasized that rebuffing your dog, as pointed out, does nothing more than a bad memory for you and your dog. In such situations, it is ideal to leave, quiet down, and next arrangement a positive way to deal with work with your dog's behavior.

Before we choose that encouraging feedback training is the way to go, how about we make a stride back and truly consider when negative reinforcement training can be utilized in a non-injurious design as a way to show your dog. To all the more likely express this present, how about we consider one thing that you like or appreciate; for instance, of this, maybe you genuinely thank eating fish. Presently, this could sound huge, however how about we express that anytime you expend an excessive amount of fish at one go, your stomach won't feel that great a while later. Sometimes, however, you can't withstand the hankering to stuff yourself with fish, and as a consequence, you experience the ill effects of looseness of the bowels. Does this make you "wrong?" I figure the vast majority would consent that the appropriate response is unquestionably not.

Presently, use a similar circumstance to your dog. Perhaps your dog truly appreciates burrowing holes, and although he is well-prepared, there might be times where he truly needs to dive caverns in your greenhouse. Similarly, this does not mean your dog is an "awful" dog. At times, for example, these, times where your dog shows a specific determined behavior, one thing that should be possible is utilizing negative reinforcements with the goal that you can divert your dog's reaction to something proper to you. Returning to a similar model, whenever you see your dog beginning to dive holes in your patio, one could state something, for example, "Eh, Jasper (your dog's name), come here." This helps monitor your dog's behavior and reminds your dog that the action that he is attempting to endeavor is a no go. Once more, the point here isn't to compromise your dog, yet somewhat, to control your dog in the course of different things that he acknowledges which can be achieved with bad behavior (uplifting feedback). Intruding on the actions of your dog won't just impact your dog to keep away from such responses within a reasonable time-frame, yet by doing as such in a non-oppressive way, you won't prompt dread into your dog.

So more or less, uplifting feedback training is without a doubt the way to go; notwithstanding the idea that at times, dog owners need to blend it up by including certain sorts of non-damaging negative reinforcement training.

Basic Dog Commands - Training a Puppy

Everything in life needs to create and make. This applies to our associations too. This furthermore applies to our relationship with our canines. Despite whether you just got your finished nearest friend and need to plant the seeds of an agreeable long term connection, or you have been living individually for quite a while, and need to take your relationship to the accompanying level, we all in all need course every so often. Besides, many equivalents to you would go to an expert if that you required progressively out of your relationship with your associate, you would go to a... pooch preparing school if you expected to wear down your relationship with your canine.

The request is, how might you find an average master? By and by, if you were feeling wiped out, you would in all probability go to a general master. Regardless, envision a situation where you had a toothache. I bet you would go to a dental master! Same with canine preparing. To start with, you need to pick whether you have to tackle general consistency, antagonistic vibe, division apprehension, or maybe you have to take on treatment pooch preparing or a security canine instructional class. What's more, from that point forward, you got the chance to examine on because we made a summary of adjacent covered pearls in San Diego zone that invest noteworthy energy inaccurately the kind of canine instructional courses you need!

By and by, what kinds of pooch preparing schools would we say we are going to look at definitely?

Pooch Obedience Training

Compelling Dog Training;

Guard Dog Training or Security Dog Training;

Conduct Modification Dog Training - Dog Separation Anxiety Training;

Treatment Dog Training

Organization Dog Training

We will, in like manner, examine such preparing sorts as a canine preparing camp, bunch classes, in-home pooch preparing, and online canine preparing.

These jewels have 5-star evaluations on Yelp, enormous measures of cheery clients and they are adjacent, for the most part, family-guaranteed associations, so you can make mind-boggling sidekicks among your neighbors while doing some preparation as well!

Above all else, there is a lot of decisions out there concerning pooch preparing. How might you know which one is valuable for you? Here are six indications.

For Picking the Right Dog Training School;

1. Understand That the Dog Training Industry is Unregulated

That suggests that in every practical sense, anyone could see oneself as a coach, lamentably. Regardless, a few confirmations and affiliations can empower you to recognize the people who have the right assignments and experience. Ceaselessly check whether the coach has a part of the going with accreditations

2. Know the Training Methods Used

By and by, all coaches have distinctive preparing strategies, yet here are several crucial things that would empower you to swim absolutely in the sea of mentor language. There are at present four essential techniques for preparing that originate from conduct brain science: uplifting feedback, negative support, positive discipline, and negative control. By and by, the words positive and negative aren't addressing the possibility of "good and vindictiveness" here, they work progressively as they would in math, with positive significance extension and negative centrality subtraction of something. It will advance toward ending up progressively evident in a second.

Encouraging feedback

This is the most outstanding technique today, and, sure enough, you are, generally, familiar with it. Encouraging feedback has, at its middle, repaying a canine for wanted conduct commonly with a treat, a toy or recess, dependent upon what influences your pooch the most. Attempt to pick the right arranging: correspondingly, as your canine does the ideal conduct, repay that individual promptly, and supplement the treatment with a sharp "conventional pooch," to guarantee your pet recognizes how fulfilled you are with this conduct. See how a treat is incorporated here? This is the positive part, the development.

Negative Reinforcement

This framework incorporates evacuating something appalling to reinforce the ideal conduct. That is how electrical divider work, for example. At the point when a canine gets too much close to the fringe, it receives a shock, yet the stagger disappears the moment the pooch moves from the cutoff. This way, the pooch makes sense of how to keep away from the fringe. See the subtraction here - the loathsome sensations are evacuated to sustain conduct, this is negative support.

Positive Punishment

With discipline strategies, the coach is endeavoring to make particular conduct happen less consistently. With positive discipline, the coach adds some unpleasant enhancements to cripple a tone. With over the top woofing, for example, a mentor can add a sprinkle bark neck area to the preparation, so every time a canine barks, it gets showered. The pooch will relate inconvenience woofing with being sprinkled, and this will cripple the individual being referred to from yapping for the duration of the night yet again. Did you see how with this strategy a mentor would incorporate (=positive) something to debilitate conduct (=punishment)?

Negative Punishment

This framework construes evacuating something (=negative) to cripple conduct (=punishment). A certifiable model will be if a mentor gets some good ways from a pooch that is bobbing on him or different people to get through. He expels the consideration from the canine to weaken undesired conduct. This technique is consistently used together with uplifting feedback to diminish the unfortunate manner and strengthen the ideal activity.

Alright, that was a lot of information, isn't that so? Did it become, somewhat, progressively clear what the diverse preparing techniques do? Astounding. There is still much discourse around the best preparing strategies in the coaches' world, yet what you lift keeps awake to you.

Directly that you've gotten acquainted with the social brain science, do you start seeing a couple of comparable qualities between how we train canines and how the organization trains us? On to the accompanying tip.